P9-CFD-837

A Robbie Reader

What's So Great About . . . ?

GEORGE WASHINGTON CARVER

Amie Jane Leavitt

Mitchell Lane
PUBLISHERS

P.O. Box 196
Hockessin, Delaware 19707
Visit us on the web: www.mitchelllane.com
Comments? email us: mitchelllane@mitchelllane.com

Mitchell Lane
PUBLISHERS

Printing   1   2   3   4   5   6   7   8   9

A Robbie Reader/What's So Great About . . . ?

Amelia Earhart	Anne Frank	Annie Oakley
Christopher Columbus	Daniel Boone	Davy Crockett
Elizabeth Blackwell	Ferdinand Magellan	Francis Scott Key
Galileo	**George Washington Carver**	Harriet Tubman
Helen Keller	Henry Hudson	Jacques Cartier
Johnny Appleseed	Paul Bunyan	Robert Fulton
Rosa Parks	Sam Houston	

Library of Congress Cataloging-in-Publication Data
Leavitt, Amie Jane.
  George Washington Carver / by Amie Jane Leavitt.
      p. cm. — (A Robbie reader. What's so great about . . . ?)
  Includes bibliographical references.
  ISBN 978-1-58415-580-5 (library bound) *3755 1453 5/08*
  1. Carver, George Washington, 1864?–1943—Juvenile literature. 2. Agriculturists—United States—Biography—Juvenile literature. 3. African American agriculturists—Biography—Juvenile literature. I. Title.
S417.C3L43 2008
630.92—dc22
[B]
                                                                              2007000813

ABOUT THE AUTHOR: Amie Jane Leavitt is the author of numerous articles, puzzles, workbooks, and tests for kids and teens. She is a former teacher who has taught all subjects and grade levels. Ms. Leavitt loves to travel, play tennis, and learn new things every day. She, too, believes in following your dreams.

PHOTO CREDITS: Cover, pp. 4, 18, 22, 24—Library of Congress; pp. 1, 3, 16—Stringer/Hulton Archive/Getty Images; p. 6—GFDL; p. 8—WGBH/PBS; p. 12—NC Policy Watch; p. 15—Iowa State University; p. 21—Jupiter Images; p. 26—U.S. Department of Transportation; p. 27—FPG/Hulton Archive/Getty Images.

TABLE OF CONTENTS

Chapter One
A Day in Congress 5

Chapter Two
Plant Doctor 9

Chapter Three
A Love of Learning 13

Chapter Four
Helping the Farmers 19

Chapter Five
A Living Legacy 23

Chronology 28
Timeline in History 29
Find Out More 30
    Books 30
    Works Consulted 30
    On the Internet 30
Glossary 31
Index 32

Words in **bold** type can be found in the glossary.

George Washington Carver once said: "How far you go in life depends on your being tender with the young, compassionate with the aged, sympathetic with the striving, and tolerant of the weak and the strong. Because someday in life you will have been all of these."

A Day in Congress

George Washington Carver walked into the Capitol Building in Washington, D.C. On that day—January 20, 1921—he was giving a speech to the United States **Congress** (KON-gres). Carver was wearing an old gray suit with a flower pinned to his jacket. He carried a box of supplies.

Carver was a scientist with some extraordinary ideas. He hoped to share these ideas with the leaders of the country.

Carver wanted to talk to the leaders about peanuts. He believed this plant could help Southern farmers. For years, these farmers had relied on cotton crops to make a living. Over the years, the cotton had taken many of the

After George Washington Carver convinced the U.S. Congress that peanuts could be useful, Southern farmers began planting more of the crop.

nutrients (NOO-tree-ents) out of the soil. Carver believed that planting peanuts could make the soil healthy again.

Many Southern farmers did not want to grow peanuts. They didn't think enough people would buy them. People in the United States were already buying peanuts from other countries. The U.S. farmers could not charge enough for their peanuts to make a living.

That's why George needed the leaders' help. He needed them to pass a tariff, or tax, on peanuts that were brought into the United States from other countries. Then Southern farmers would be able to sell more of their peanuts. If they could sell more, they would grow more. They could earn a living, and at the same time, the soil could recover.

At first, the leaders didn't think the tariff was a good idea. Although peanut butter was becoming popular, they didn't think the farmers would be able to sell very many peanuts.

Carver reached into his box of supplies. He had been working with peanuts in his laboratory and had developed many different products made from them. He showed the leaders some of these products, such as shaving cream, wood stains, flour, soap, plastics, ink, and shampoo.

The leaders could not believe their eyes. None of them had ever imagined that peanuts could be so useful. They all agreed that this crop could be important after all. Later, the leaders voted to pass a tariff on imported peanuts. Carver had helped the farmers.

By the time George Washington Carver was born, U.S. President Abraham Lincoln had outlawed slavery in many states. However, slavers continued to take people from Africa and sell them as slaves.

Plant Doctor

George Carver was born into slavery in Missouri. He never knew his exact birthday. He only knew he was born around 1865, during the Civil War. His mother, Mary, was a slave on Moses and Susan Carver's farm. George's father had been a slave on another farm. He died in a wagon accident just before George was born. George had two older sisters and one brother, Jim. He never knew his sisters.

One night, baby George was sick with a bad cough. His mother was trying to take care of him. Suddenly, the door burst open. Some men forced Mary, George, and one of his sisters into a wagon and drove them away from the Carvers' farm. These men were slave raiders. They were going to sell Mary and her children to other slave owners.

The Carvers searched for them everywhere. They finally found George and brought him home. They never found Mary or his sister. At a very young age, George and Jim were **orphans** (OR-fins). They were raised by Moses and Susan Carver. George called them Aunt and Uncle.

Moses and Susan Carver were **immigrants** (IH-mih-grunts) from Germany. They had moved to Missouri to buy a farm. "Mr. and Mrs. Carver were very kind to me," George said later. "They encouraged me to secure knowledge, helping me all they could." They treated George and Jim like family.

George was often in poor health. He didn't have the strength to work in the fields like Jim. Instead, he helped Susan around the house. He cleaned dishes, cooked meals, knitted socks, and washed clothes. He even helped in the garden—his favorite activity.

As a child, George loved everything about nature. He spent hours outside looking at plants. "Day after day I spent in the woods alone to collect my floral beauties and put them in my little garden," he remembered. George studied the roots, leaves, and flowers of these plants. He saw things that other people didn't notice. He knew that some plants needed lots of water. He knew that some plants needed soft soil. George grew his own plants in a special place in the woods. He would take sick plants there to help them get better.

"Many are the tears I have shed because I would break the roots or flowers of some of my pets while removing them from the ground, and strange to say all sorts of **vegetation** [veh-jeh-TAY-shun] seemed to thrive under my touch," he said.

Soon, people heard about George's talent with plants. They called him the Plant Doctor. George was proud that people would call him such an important name.

People marching in the 1960s to gain equal rights for African Americans. Even after slavery was over in the United States, it took many years before black children could go to school with white children. Carver had trouble getting into college because of the color of his skin.

A Love of Learning

George was eleven when he asked to go to school. Aunt Susan had taught him how to read, but he wanted to learn more. There was a school in Diamond, where they lived, yet only white children could go there. The nearest school for black children was eight miles away in Neosho (nee-OH-shoh). George could not walk that far every day, so he had to move there.

George packed his bags and waved good-bye to Moses, Susan, and Jim. He didn't know where he would live. He knew he was going to school, and that was all that mattered.

When George arrived in Neosho, he was lucky to meet Mariah and Andrew Watkins. They let George live with them while he went to school. They only asked George to help with the chores to earn his room and meals.

George worked hard in school. He even studied during recess! At home, after he finished his chores, he would read late into the night.

George stayed at this school for four years. By that time, he knew everything his teacher did. He had also read all the books there. It was time for George to move on to a more difficult school. The closest one was in Kansas, so George had to move again. He was sad to say good-bye to the kind Watkinses.

In Kansas, George did many odd jobs while he attended school. He worked as a cook, and he washed clothes. Once again, he tried to read every book he could find. In high school, he gave himself the middle name of Washington.

Iowa Agricultural College, where Carver studied botany. Carver, a talented painter, began his college years studying art and music. However, he said, "With a knowledge of agriculture I can be of greater service to my race."

George **graduated** (GRAD-jooh-way-ted) from high school in 1884. His **diploma** (dih-PLOH-muh) had the name George Washington Carver on it.

After high school, George wanted to go to college. He was accepted to Highland College in Kansas. Yet when he arrived, he received some upsetting news. The principal told George that he was smart enough to go to the college, but he would not be allowed to attend because he was black.

Carver in a university laboratory. He took his first teaching job in 1894. He would continue to teach students and farmers for the rest of his life.

George was very sad. He gave up his dream of college for a while. He started his own small farm in Kansas. He studied plants and helped his neighbors with their crops. Yet he soon grew tired of this life. He knew he should be doing more. He stayed on his farm for only a few years.

George applied for college again. In 1890, he was accepted to Simpson College in Iowa. This school didn't care about his skin color. The people there only cared that he was a good student and wanted to learn. George studied art and music there, and then moved to another school in Iowa. Finally, in 1894, he graduated from Iowa **Agricultural** (aa-grih-KUL-chuh-rul) College. The school offered him a job. He became the first African American to teach at what would someday be called Iowa State University.

In April 1896, Booker T. Washington wrote Carver a letter. He wanted Carver to come teach science at the Tuskegee Institute. In the letter, he said: "I cannot offer you money, position or fame. The first two you have. The last, from the place you now occupy, you will no doubt achieve. These things I now ask you to give up. I offer you in their place work—hard, hard work—the task of bringing a people from degradation [deh-greh-DAY-shun], poverty and waste to full manhood."

Helping the Farmers

One day, a famous African American named Booker T. Washington visited Carver. He wanted Carver to work at a school for African Americans called the Tuskegee (TUS-keh-gee) Institute. Carver wouldn't make much money, but he would be able to teach people how to farm and take care of plants.

It wasn't long before Booker T. Washington knew he had made the right choice. He said that Carver was "a great teacher, a great lecturer, a great inspirer of young men and old men."

Carver knew that students learn best by trying things out for themselves. He once said,

"The thoughtful educator realizes that a very large part of education must be gotten outside the four walls of the classroom." As much as possible, he took his students outdoors to study plants.

He also wanted to teach the local farmers how to grow better crops. A lot of farmers in the South were struggling to make money during this time period. Carver felt he could do something to help.

Most farmers in the South grew cotton. Before the Civil War, this crop had made people rich. Yet cotton was very hard on the soil. It removed all the nutrients. Soon, the cotton wouldn't grow anymore. The farmers had a hard time making any money to feed their families.

Carver taught the farmers that to build up the soil again, they needed to grow other things. He told them to grow peanuts.

The farmers just laughed at this. Why would they want to grow peanuts? Peanuts were not very popular. The farmers did not believe they could make much money growing them.

Carver believed differently. He knew that all plants were useful. He spent time in his **laboratory** (LAA-bruh-tor-ee) to prove it. He did **experiments** (ex-PEER-ih-ments) on the peanuts. He wanted to find out how else they could be used.

One night, George invited the farmers to a feast. He prepared many delicious dishes. The farmers told George how much they loved the food. After everyone finished eating, George told them his secret. All the food was made from peanuts.

The farmers couldn't believe it! If peanuts were this useful, then maybe growing them would be a good idea after all.

In a radio address in 1941, Carver recalled traveling from Iowa to Alabama: "When my train left the golden wheat fields and the tall green corn of Iowa for the acres of cotton, nothing but cotton, my heart sank. . . . The scraggly cotton grew close up to the cabin doors; a few lonesome collards, the only sign of vegetables. . . . Everything looked hungry: the land, the cotton, the cattle, and the people."

A Living Legacy

George Washington Carver wasn't just a scientist. He was also a musician and an artist. He could play the piano very well, and he was a talented painter. His specialty was painting nature pictures. He made his own paint colors using soil, rocks, and flower petals. He had other talents too. "I knit, I crochet, and made all my hose, mittens . . . while I was in school," he once told a friend.

Carver worked his entire life to help others. "Some day I will have to leave this world. And when that day comes, I want to feel that I have an excuse for having lived in it. I want to feel that my life has been of some service to my fellow man," he said in 1917.

Carver didn't care about riches. He took only a small **salary** (SAA-luh-ree) from Tuskegee. He once said, "I've never received any money for my discoveries. Somebody who had benefited by one of my products from the

George Washington Carver, seated in the bottom row in the middle, with other staff members from Tuskegee. Besides teaching at the school, Carver traveled the countryside and taught the farmers. His work helped change the lives of the people in the South.

peanut sent me $100 the other day, but I sent it back to him."

Carver dressed in old suits. "It is not the style of clothes one wears, neither the kind of automobile one drives, nor the amount of money one has in the bank, that counts. These mean nothing. It is simply service that measures success," he once said. Even though Carver dressed plainly, he always had a fresh flower pinned to his suit jacket.

Many important people had nice things to say about Carver. "Professor Carver has taken Thomas Edison's place as the world's greatest living scientist," said automaker Henry Ford near the end of Carver's life. In 1937, *Life* magazine named George "one of the great scientists of the U.S."

Carver experimented with many types of plants, including sweet potatoes. This popular food is also healthy for the soil.

George Washington Carver died on January 5, 1943. When Franklin D. Roosevelt—President of the United States—heard the news, he was sad. "The world of science has lost one of its most **eminent** [EH-mih-nunt] figures. All mankind," he said, would benefit from Carver's discoveries about plants and soil.

During his lifetime, George Washington Carver did many important things. He published books listing over 300 different uses for peanuts. He told people there were over 100 different ways to use the sweet potato. He

President Franklin D. Roosevelt respected George Washington Carver and his work in the field of science. In 1939, Carver was awarded the Roosevelt Medal for Outstanding Contribution to Southern Agriculture.

Carver shakes the hand of Edsel Ford, Henry Ford's son, in 1940. Carver helped the Ford Motor Company develop rubber for tires. They believed other car parts, including fuel, could also be made from plants.

helped farmers learn how to take better care of their land. He also helped Henry Ford learn how to use rubber from plants for car tires.

Carver never spent much money on himself, so he had a lot saved. In 1940, he used some of it to start the George Washington Carver Foundation. He left the rest of it to the Tuskegee Institute. This money helps people learn more about plants even today.

27

CHRONOLOGY

1865 George is born on Moses and Susan Carver's farm in Diamond, Missouri (exact date unknown). He and his mother are kidnapped by slave raiders (exact date unknown). Moses and Susan Carver find George and bring him home to raise (exact date unknown).

1876 George leaves the Carvers' house to begin school in Neosho, Missouri.

1884 He travels to Minneapolis, Kansas, to attend high school.

1885 He is turned away from Highland College in Kansas because he is black.

1886 He becomes a farmer in Ness County, Kansas.

1890 He enrolls at Simpson College in Iowa.

1893 He receives an award for one of his paintings at the World's Columbian Exposition in Chicago.

1894 He receives a Bachelor of Agriculture degree from Iowa Agricultural College; he becomes a professor there.

1896 He earns a master's degree in agriculture. Booker T. Washington asks him to be the director of agriculture at Tuskegee Institute in Alabama.

1919 Carver develops peanut milk.

1921 To help U.S. farmers sell their crops, Carver addresses the U.S. House Ways and Means Committee on the uses of peanuts.

1923 He receives the Spingarn Medal for Distinguished Service to Science.

1940 He establishes the George Washington Carver Museum and Foundation in Tuskegee.

1943 Carver dies in Tuskegee, Alabama, on January 5. His birthplace is made a national monument.

TIMELINE IN HISTORY

1860   Abraham Lincoln is elected president of the United States. South Carolina leaves the Union. Many other Southern states follow. The Civil War begins.

1863   Abraham Lincoln issues Emancipation Proclamation. This document frees the slaves.

1865   Civil War ends. The Thirteenth Amendment to the Constitution abolishes slavery.

1868   The Fourteenth Amendment gives U.S. citizenship to all African American men.

1870   All African American men gain the right to vote.

1881   Tuskegee Institute is founded.

1890   George A. Bayle Jr. begins selling ground peanut paste to help people with bad teeth.

1895   Dr. John Harvey Kellogg and his brother, W. K. Kellogg, make peanut butter using steamed peanuts in Battle Creek, Michigan.

1896   Supreme Court says that "separate but equal" is okay. This means that African Americans can be denied access to certain schools, hotels, restaurants, and other public places.

1904   C. H. Sumner introduces peanut butter at the Saint Louis World's Fair.

1908   Krema Products Company in Columbus, Ohio, begins selling peanut butter on a wide scale.

1914   World War I begins. It will last until 1919.

1920   The Nineteenth Amendment gives women the right to vote.

1922   Joseph L. Rosefield develops the recipe for modern smooth peanut butter.

1939   World War II begins. It will last until 1945.

1955   African Americans boycott buses in Montgomery, Alabama. The U.S. Supreme Court orders schools to teach black and white students together.

1958   Procter & Gamble introduces Jif brand peanut butter.

1964   Civil Rights Act is passed.

1967   Thurgood Marshall becomes the first African American Supreme Court Justice.

1976   Jimmy Carter, a peanut farmer from Georgia, is elected U.S. president.

1984   African American civil rights leader Jesse Jackson runs for U.S. president. He will run again in 1988.

1998   Airlines begin banning peanuts from flights to protect people who are allergic to peanuts.

2001   Colin Powell becomes the first African American in U.S. history to hold the office of secretary of state.

2005   Condoleezza Rice becomes the first African American female to become secretary of state.

2007   African American Barack Obama runs for U.S. president.

FIND OUT MORE

Books

Carter, Andy, and Carol Saller. *George Washington Carver.* Minneapolis: Carolrhoda Books, Inc., 2001.

Driscoll, Laura. *George Washington Carver: Peanut Wizard.* New York: Grosset and Dunlap, 2003.

Works Consulted

Bruchard, Peter Duncan. "George Washington Carver: For His Time and Ours." National Park Service, 2005. http://home.nps.gov/applications/parks/gwca/ppdocuments/Special%20History%20Study.pdf

Elliott, Lawrence. *George Washington Carver: The Man Who Overcame.* Englewood Cliffs, New Jersey: Prentice-Hall, Inc., 1966.

Holt, Rackham. *George Washington Carver: An American Biography.* Garden City, New York: Doubleday, Doran and Company, Inc., 1943.

Mackintosh, Barry. "George Washington Carver and the Peanut." *American Heritage Magazine,* August 1977. http://www.americanheritage.com/articles/magazine/ah/1977/5/1977_5_66.shtml

McMurry, Linda O. *George Washington Carver: Scientist and Symbol.* New York: Oxford University Press, 1981.

National Park Service: *George Washington Carver National Monument,* "1897 or Thereabouts–George Washington Carver's Own Brief History of His Life." http://www.nps.gov/gwca/expanded/auto_bio.htm

On the Internet

Iowa State University: *George Washington Carver All-University Celebration,* "The Legacy of George Washington Carver" http://www.lib.iastate.edu/spcl/gwc/bio.html

National Park Service: *The George Washington Carver National Monument* http://www.nps.gov/archive/gwca/expanded/main.htm

GLOSSARY

agricultural (aa-grih-KUL-chuh-rul)—Having to do with crop farming.

congress (KON-gres)—The part of the government that makes laws.

diploma (dih-PLOH-muh)—An official piece of paper that says someone has finished school.

eminent (EH-mih-nunt)—Standing at the top in one's field.

experiments (ex-PEER-ih-ments)—A carefully planned test to discover something unknown.

graduated (GRAD-jooh-way-ted)—Finished school.

immigrants (IH-mih-grunts)—People who move to a new country.

laboratory (LAA-bruh-tor-ee)—A place used for scientific experiments.

nutrients (NOO-tree-ents)—The parts of food that help people, animals, and plants live and grow.

orphan (OR-fin)—A child whose parents have both died.

salary (SAA-luh-ree)—Money earned for a steady job.

vegetation (veh-jeh-TAY-shun)—Plant life.

INDEX

Africa 8

Carver, George Washington
 4, 22
  awards for 25, 26
  birth of 9
  death of 26
  childhood of 9–11, 13–15
  education of 12, 14–15, 17
  experiments of 7, 16, 21
  hobbies of 10, 11, 23
  parents of 9
  speaks to U.S. Congress
   5–7
  as teacher 16, 17, 19–20,
   24
Carver, Jim (brother) 9, 10, 13
Carver, Mary (mother) 9, 10
Carver, Moses (guardian) 9,
 10, 13
Carver, Susan (guardian) 9,
 10, 13
Civil War 9, 20
cotton 5, 20, 22
Diamond, Missouri 13

Ford, Edsel 27
Ford, Henry 25, 27
fuel 27
George Washington Carver
  Foundation 27
Highland College 15
Iowa Agricultural College 15,
 17
Kansas 14
Lincoln, Abraham 8
Neosho, Missouri 13, 14
peanuts 5–7, 20–21
Plant Doctor 11
Roosevelt, Franklin D. 26
rubber 27
Simpson College 17
slave raiders 9–10
slavery 8, 9–10, 12
sweet potatoes 25, 27
Tuskegee Institute 18, 24
Washington, Booker T. 18, 19
Watkins, Andrew 14
Watkins, Mariah 14